STUDY GUIDE

The Doctrines of
Grace in John

Steven J. Lawson

LIGONIER MINISTRIES

Renew your Mind.

LIGONIER.ORG | 800-435-4343

1

Laying the Foundation

MESSAGE INTRODUCTION

Each book of the Bible contributes poignantly and uniquely to the message of redemption revealed in God's Word. John's gospel offers much to the picture of redemption, but it provides special insight into the deity and supremacy of Jesus Christ. For this reason, it naturally follows that John would present the sovereignty of God in a profound, thorough manner. Therefore, Dr. Lawson will use the Beloved's record of the life and ministry of Jesus, the all-mighty Son of God, to explain and analyze the doctrines of grace, and he begins his lecture series with an introduction to John's gospel and its insight into these doctrines.

SCRIPTURE READINGS

Exodus 3:13–15; John 1:1–18; 3:1–21; 4:14, 42; 5:24; 6; 28–59; 7:37; 10; 11:26; 15:16; 20:30–31

LEARNING OBJECTIVES

1. To understand the unique contribution of John's gospel to the biblical corpus and Christian thought
2. To recognize the dual focus of his gospel: the free offer of the gospel and the sovereignty of God in salvation
3. To get acquainted with the doctrines of grace

QUOTATION

And so that which is said 'God wills all men to be saved' though He is unwilling that so many be saved, is said for this reason: that all who are saved, are not saved except by His will.

—St. Augustine of Hippo

LECTURE OUTLINE

I. Introduction
    a. The gospel of John has an enormous amount to say on the subject of biblical Calvinism and the doctrines of grace. Its lofty perspective on salvation makes it a perfect place from which to trace the five main headings of the doctrines of grace.
    b. Three questions need addressing in this first lesson.
        i.   What is the unique focus of John's gospel?
        ii. What two issues does the book primarily address?
        iii. What are the doctrines of grace?

II. The Unique Focus of John's Gospel
    a. Every book of the Bible contributes uniquely to the biblical corpus.
        i.   John, in marked contrast to the other Gospels, presents the deity and supremacy of Christ in a breathtaking manner.
        ii. All of the Gospels address and elucidate both natures of the person of Christ (human and divine), but whereas the Synoptic Gospels emphasize Jesus' humanity, John focuses on his divinity.
    b. The content of the book of John demonstrates a special attention to God's sovereignty as befits His deity.
        i.   The prologue of John presents His eternality and the fullness of His deity.
        ii. The seven "I Am" statements reinforce His transcendence as God.

III. The Dual Focuses of John's Gospel
    a. The book portrays the offer of the gospel as free and unbiased.
        i.   Numerous passages attest to this unequivocal call (e.g. John 4:14, 42, etc.).
        ii. The invitation to repent and believe addresses all people, wherever they might reside (John 3:16; 6:51, etc.).
        iii. Jesus will not reject anyone who responds to the call, but He who came to seek and to save welcomes faith (John 6:37; 7:37, etc.).
    b. The book presents salvation as under the sovereignty of God.
        i.   These two focuses do not contradict each other.
            1. The Bible depicts these truths as compatible, and we must accept them as such, despite our inability to fully grasp their relation.
            2. This occurs in Scripture often, and you don't just throw out one because of the other. You accept them as truth, recognizing the finitude of the human mind.
        ii. John offers ample evidence for God's sovereignty in salvation.
            1. God must instigate and create a new, spiritual birth, similar to His role in physical birth (John 3).

2. God controls the hearts of men and chooses whom to give to Christ. (John 6:37, etc.).
3. No man can institute this change in his heart, but God must quicken life in the heart before one may accept the call, join the flock of Christ, and follow His voice for all eternity (John 10; 11:26).

IV. The Doctrines of Grace

   a. The doctrines of grace (the focus of this lecture series) set forth the glory of God's saving grace. They are titled as follows: 1. Radical Depravity 2. Sovereign Election 3. Definite Atonement 4. Irresistible Call 5. Persevering Grace.
   b. The gospel of John teaches these doctrines clearly and irrefutably.
   c. The doctrines stand and fall together, and their interwoven nature necessitates their complete acceptance or rejection.
   d. The doctrines elevate God while humbling man.
      i. Man remains dead in His trespasses until God pulls him from this state.
      ii. This emphasis demonstrates the amazing grace demonstrated by our high, lofty God, a God who would reach across the chasm of sin to reconcile us to Himself. John's gospel, maybe more than any other, demonstrates for us God's mind-boggling, jaw-dropping grace

STUDY QUESTIONS

1. The gospel of John and the book of _____ feature the sovereignty of God in salvation more than any other.
   a. Philippians
   b. Psalms
   c. Hebrews
   d. Romans

2. Matthew, Mark, and Luke do not present on the deity of Christ at all, but they attend solely to His humanity.
   a. True
   b. False

3. The prologue of the gospel of John demonstrates the fullness of His deity, an important emphasis of the book.
   a. True
   b. False

4. The message of the gospel goes out to _____.
    a. everyone, everywhere
    b. only a select few, everywhere
    c. everyone, only in a few locations
    d. no one

5. If we cannot reconcile certain doctrines clearly advocated in the Word of God, they must be mutually exclusive.
    a. True
    b. False

6. When Jesus describes the wind in John 3, he does so to demonstrate _____.
    a. man's ability to accept the call of the gospel
    b. God's sovereign role in regeneration
    c. the importance of nature in creation
    d. the unpredictability of God

7. The doctrines of grace elevate God and humble man, highlighting the amazing grace involved in salvation.
    a. True
    b. False

BIBLE STUDY AND DISCUSSION QUESTIONS

1. Can you name the unique focuses of some of the other books of the Bible? Genesis? Proverbs? Colossians? Revelation? Choose a few books, provide the unique focuses, and explain your answers.

2. Explain the importance of a presentation both of Christ's humanity and His deity. What would we lose with out one or the other?

3. Explain, as best you can, the incarnation of the Son of God. How many natures does Jesus Christ possess? Use Scripture for support.

4. Does the doctrine of God's sovereign election exclude the free call of the gospel, or vice versa? Define the two doctrines and explain your answer. Provide biblical evidence for your position.

5. How does the imagery of birth contribute to understanding God's sovereignty in salvation?

6. Does the sovereignty of God in salvation make evangelism moot and unnecessary?

7.　Why must the doctrines of grace be accepted as a whole and not piecemeal? Explain the role of grace in them.

SUGGESTED READING FOR FURTHER STUDY

Calvin, John. *The Institutes of Christian Religion*

Horton, Michael. *Putting Amazing Back into Grace: Embracing the Heart of the Gospel*

Sproul, R.C. *What Is Reformed Theology?*

Steele, David N., Thomas, Curtis C., Quinn, Lance S. *The Five Points of Calvinism: Defined, Defended, and Documented*

2

Radical Depravity (Part 1)

MESSAGE INTRODUCTION

How often do we hear in our culture the adage, "He or she has a good heart"? This attribution of an innate, inherent goodness occurs frequently, and it demonstrates the general, common belief that mankind, despite his clear, unequivocal iniquity, ultimately is good. Contrary to this proposal, the Word of God paints a significantly different picture of the nature of humanity. Jesus declares (drawing from the Old Testament) to the rich young ruler in Matthew 19 that no one is good except for God, and He elaborates on man's condition by asserting that humanity cannot reverse their position unaided. This lesson on the first doctrine of grace, radical depravity, explains and explores mankind's sinful, depraved state.

SCRIPTURE READINGS

Psalm 14:1–3; John 1:1–18; 3:1–21, 36; 5:24–30; Romans 3:9–20; 1 Corinthians 2:14; 2 Corinthians 4:3–4; Ephesians 2:1; Colossians 2:12–13

LEARNING OBJECTIVES

1. To understand properly the radical state of spiritual death in which natural man resides
2. To recognize that this spiritual deadness creates ignorance, blindness, hatred, and defiance against Jesus, as well as the inability to accept the free call of the gospel

QUOTATION

Not only the worst of my sins but the best of my duties speak me a child of Adam.

—William Beveridge

LECTURE OUTLINE

I. Radical Depravity

    a. Sometimes called total depravity

    b. This forms the first part of our focus because we need to understand humanity's condition before God's intervention.

    c. Radical depravity means that the entirety of a human being suffers from the plague and death of sin. This curse afflicts all of mankind, and it begins with Adam's fall and is transferred to his progeny.

    d. The gospel of John provides a striking picture of man's depravity before God.

II. Man's Depravity Creates Spiritual Ignorance.

    a. Sin has darkened the mind of every person born into this world (excluding Jesus).

        i. John 1:1–9: Jesus is the light, yet the world does not know Him.

            1. Despite the fact that no man had ever lived a life of holiness and perfection as Jesus did, the world did not recognize Him as the Son of God.

            2. Even if Jesus appeared amongst humanity today, it would still not acknowledge His deity.

    b. Recognition of Jesus occurs only through the life-giving activity of God.

        i. The Lord veils His gospel to natural man (1 Cor. 2:14; 2 Cor. 4:3–4, etc.).

        ii. Acceptance of the free call requires a dramatic change of heart engendered by God.

III. Man's Depravity Creates Spiritual Blindness.

    a. Humanity cannot see the truth of Christ in its depraved condition.

        i. John 3:3: "Unless one is born again, he cannot see the kingdom of heaven."

        ii. This involves ability, not permission

    b. Rebirth and consequent proper sight demands the Holy Spirit's activity.

IV. Man's Depravity Creates Enmity toward Jesus Christ.

    a. John 3:19–20: There exists in the heart of man spiritual hatred toward Jesus Christ.

        i. This hatred results from God's judgment on sin.

        ii. The hatred takes the form of both active rebellion and passive indifference.

    b. Depraved man abhors Christ all the more because He fears that the light of Christ will expose his evil practices in the darkness.

V. Man's Depravity Creates Spiritual Defiance.

    a. All those in a state of spiritual unbelief disobey God.

    i. John 3:36: the wrath of God abides in the unbeliever.

    ii. God's wrath responds to disobedience.

  b. The gospel goes forth as a command, not a request, and the depraved man shuns this command with venom.

VI. Man's Depravity Creates Spiritual Death.

  a. All those outside of Christ exist in a state of spiritual death (John 5:25; Eph. 2:1; Col. 2:12–13).

    i. Depraved man does not possess some sickness capable of curing through the use of antidotes.

    ii. On the contrary, spiritual death reigns over the natural man, and a dead man does not possess any capability other than to rot and stink.

  b. Spiritual resurrection must occur before man might live.

STUDY QUESTIONS

1. The notion of radical depravity confines man's sinfulness to the body alone.
  a. True
  b. False

2. If the Incarnation of Jesus Christ occurred in this day and age, natural man would _____.
  a. accept Him as the savior gladly
  b. still be blind to His deity
  c. treat Him very well but not believe
  d. not know what to think

3. Natural man has permission to accept the free call of the gospel.
  a. True
  b. False

4. Natural man, according to John 3, hates the light because it _____.
  a. exposes his sin
  b. hurts his eyes
  c. forces him to follow his true nature
  d. doesn't make sense to him

5. Christ commands that man accept His call to repentance and faith.
  a. True
  b. False

6. Natural man remains in a state of spiritual _____ before regeneration.
    a. bliss
    b. limbo
    c. ambivalence
    d. death

BIBLE STUDY AND DISCUSSION QUESTIONS

1. Explain the doctrine of radical depravity. Use Scripture both inside and outside the book of John to demonstrate this doctrine's validity.

2. Why do people so vehemently object to the doctrine of radical depravity? Where might they find their support in Scripture? How would you respond?

3. How does Adam act as our federal representative in the Garden of Eden? Is it unfair that his progeny enter into this world as sinners on account of his actions? Explain.

4. Why does accepting the doctrine of radical depravity demonstrate your position on the other doctrines of grace?

5. Explain the Bible's description of Jesus Christ as the true light.

6. Why does God "blind the minds of the unbelieving"? Does this prove Him unfair and merciless? Explain.

7. Explain the difference between permission to accept the free call of the gospel and ability to accept it.

8. How does the doctrine of radical depravity raise compassion in the heart of the believer?

SUGGESTED READING FOR FURTHER STUDY

Calvin, John. *The Institutes of Christian Religion*
Horton, Michael. *Putting Amazing Back into Grace: Embracing the Heart of the Gospel*
Sproul, R.C. *Chosen by God*
Steele, David N., Thomas, Curtis C., Quinn, Lance S. *The Five Points of Calvinism: Defined, Defended, and Documented*

3

Radical Depravity (Part 2)

MESSAGE INTRODUCTION

Understanding the true depth of man's fallen nature can arouse a shudder, but sadness and fear should not remain the final response. On the contrary, properly understanding the depravity of man's condition leads to a correct and exalted view of the true grace of God in salvation. Dr. Lawson continues to explain man's spiritual tragedy in this lecture, and he encourages us to respond in thankfulness and to bestow compassion upon the lost, for if not for the grace of God, we too would remain in bondage to sin and Satan.

SCRIPTURE READINGS

Psalm 14:1–3; John 1:1–18; 3:1–21, 36; 5:24–30; 6:41–71; 8:31–47; Romans 3:9–20; 1 Corinthians 2:14; 2 Corinthians 4:3–4; Ephesians 2:1, 5, 13; Colossians 2:12–13

LEARNING OBJECTIVES

1. To understand properly the radical state of spiritual death in which natural man resides
2. To recognize that natural man does not have the spiritual ability to accept the call of Christ, exists in spiritual bondage to sin and Satan, and remains spiritually deaf

QUOTATION

Nothing pleases man more than the sort of alluring talk that tickles the pride that itches his very marrow. But however great such commendation of human excellence is . . . it so deceives as to drive those who assent to it into utter ruin.

—John Calvin

LECTURE OUTLINE

I.   The Spiritual Deadness of Natural Man

    a.   A spiritual dead man, like a corpse, contributes nothing to his own salvation (John 5:25).

        i.   Those trapped in their trespasses and sins are spiritually dead.

        ii. Although the permission to receive the call of the gospel exists, the spiritually dead does not possess the ability, for their entire being remains mortified.

    b.   As with Ezekiel and the valley of dry bones, the power of the Holy Spirit must work in the inanimate corpses of the spiritual dead to engender life.

II. Man's Depravity Creates Spiritual Inability.

    a.   John 6:44ff: No one can place their belief in Jesus as the savior without instigation by the Holy Spirit.

    b.   John 15:5: "Apart from Me, you can do nothing" (John 6:66).

III. Man's Depravity Creates Spiritual Bondage to Sin.

    a.   John 8:34: Everyone who sins remains in the bondage of slavery to sin.

        i.   The slave must obey his master.

        ii.   The slave must respond to the demands of his master.

        iii. No other master holds authority over the slave.

    b.   Only the Son can set a slave to sin free, but a slave cannot serve two masters.

IV. Man's Depravity Creates Spiritual Bondage to Satan.

    a.   John 8:44: Natural man is born into the family of Satan.

    b.   He remains of his father the Devil until the intervention of the Holy Spirit (2 Cor. 4; Eph.2:2; 1Tim. 2:26).

V.   Man's Depravity Creates Spiritual Deafness.

    a.   John 8:43, 47: Natural man cannot hear with understanding the free call of the gospel.

    b.   Although natural man physically receive the mandate to repent and believe in Jesus Christ, only the Holy Spirit can institute proper understanding in the heart of man.

STUDY QUESTIONS

1.   Jesus uses the words "truly, truly" to _____.

    a.   express the importance of the words to follow

    b.   call attention to a joke

    c.   confuse people

    d.   veil his thoughts

2. Jesus explains in John 6 that a very few can believe in Him without assistance.
    a. True
    b. False

3. Upon hearing Jesus assertion that apart from Him, no one can do anything, John records in chapter six of his gospel that many of his disciples _____ .
    a. agreed and departed
    b. left disgruntled
    c. cheered "Hosanna"
    d. agreed and convinced more to follow Him

4. Natural man exists in bondage to _____ .
    a. God
    b. the intellect
    c. sin and Satan
    d. the earth

5. Jesus did not refer to the Jews as sons of their "father the Devil" because they were His ethnic brothers and sisters and the people of God.
    a. True
    b. False

6. There are more than two spiritual families in this world.
    a. True
    b. False

7. When Jesus says, "He who has ears to hear, let him hear," He expects everyone within audible distance to understand His message.
    a. True
    b. False

BIBLE STUDY AND DISCUSSION QUESTIONS

1. Do human beings have freedom of the will? Explain, and use Scripture to support your answer.

2. If mankind possesses freedom of the will, what repercussions does this create? What does this mean for the sovereignty of God?

3. Read Ezekiel 36. What does this passage tell us about the sovereignty of God in salvation and the spiritual condition of natural man? Why do people have such a hard time accepting this?

4. How did Jesus respond when His message of divine sovereignty in salvation received criticism? Explain His reaction.

5. What does it mean for natural man to exist in bondage to sin and to Satan? Why did the religious leaders take such offense when Jesus called them sons of Satan?

6. Why did Jesus bother to preach to people who did not "have ears to hear"?

7. Explain the purpose and message of John 3:16. Why does this verse hold a place of controversy in interpretation?

SUGGESTED READING FOR FURTHER STUDY

Calvin, John. *The Institutes of Christian Religion*
Horton, Michael. *Putting Amazing Back into Grace: Embracing the Heart of the Gospel*
Sproul, R.C. *Chosen by God*
Steele, David N., Thomas, Curtis C., Quinn, Lance S. *The Five Points of Calvinism: Defined, Defended, and Documented*

4

Sovereign Election (Part 1)

MESSAGE INTRODUCTION

The doctrine of sovereign election, when viewed in an improper perspective, may seem cold and unfeeling, depicting God as callous and arbitrary in His election of some and not others. Yet, this viewpoint fails in two significant ways. First, it assumes man deserves God's favor. Second, it does not recognize the extreme love demonstrated by God toward His Son and His elect. Election finds its root in God's love, and as Dr. Lawson explains in this lesson, far from being a dictatorial, meaningless activity by an unfeeling God, sovereign election expresses the fullness of God's love for a sinful, unrepentant people unable to make the choice to love God for themselves.

SCRIPTURE READINGS

Jeremiah 1:5; John 1:1–18; 6:37–39; 10:1–21; Romans 9:1–27; 11:36; 1 Thessalonians 1:4; 2 Thessalonians 2:13; Titus 1:1; 1 Peter 1:1; 2 Peter 1:10

LEARNING OBJECTIVES

1. To understand God's authoritative, sovereign role in the election of sinners to salvation, a choice He made in eternity past
2. To recognize that this choice remains rooted in the love of the Father for His Son and for His elect

QUOTATION

Praise God for the "buts" in the Bible.

—Martyn Lloyd-Jones

LECTURE OUTLINE

I. God's Divine Choice
   a. God's divine choice to elect some for salvation originated with Him from eternity past for His own glory.
   b. John 1:12–13: Man's reception of the free call of the gospel occurs only as a result of the will of God.
       i.   The concept of birth in verse 13 refers to a spiritual birth, and it demonstrates the inactivity on the part of man, just like physical birth.
       ii. Man does not suddenly will to choose God as Savior, but God exercises His will for the salvation of men who remain dead in their trespasses (Eph. 1:4; Rom. 9:16)

II. God's Loving Choice
   a. John 6:37–39: Sovereign election remains rooted in God's love for His Son and His elect, whom He determined to save from eternity past for an inheritance for His Son.
       i.   The word "all" in verse 37 refers to all the elect.
       ii.   The activity of giving precedes the coming of the Son.
       iii. The Son cherishes and loves the gift given to Him by the Father: the elect.
   b. Verses testifying to sovereign election: Jeremiah 1:5; Romans 9:11; 1 Thessalonians 1:4; 2 Thessalonians 2:13; Titus 1:1; 1 Peter 1:1; 2 Peter 1:10

III. God's Previous Choice
   a. John 10: The flock of Christ belongs to Him long before the sheep come to Jesus by responding to His voice.
       i.   Only Jesus, the true Shepherd, possess the right to enter in through the door guarded by the gatekeeper (perhaps John the Baptist).
       ii.   The image of the sheepfold encompasses all people, not just the elect.
       iii. When the sheep that God has given to Jesus hear His voice, they separate from the unelected and follow Him.
   b. Jesus calls each member of His flock by name.
       i.   Zacchaeus, Lazarus, and other instances demonstrate Jesus' personal call.
       ii.   The personal nature of sovereign election should arouse humility in the believer, for this destiny of salvation occurs without any personal volition or will.

STUDY QUESTIONS

1. God elects some upon which to confer salvation because these people possess good in their heart.
    a. True
    b. False

2. The idea of God's sovereignty in salvation did not develop until after the apostolic era.
    a. True
    b. False

3. John 1:12–13 demonstrates the initiative of _____ in salvation.
    a. man's will
    b. God's will
    c. the angels
    d. Satan

4. God's sovereign choice to bring sinners into salvation is rooted in _____.
    a. His love for His Son and chosen
    b. the hearts of men
    c. His mercy
    d. His power

5. The word "all" used in John 6:37 refer to _____.
    a. all people
    b. all who would have good hearts
    c. all the elect
    d. all would accept Him of their own volition

6. In John 10, Jesus refers to the _____ as thiefs and robbers.
    a. the religious leaders of Israel
    b. sinners
    c. the apostles
    d. the political zealots of the day

BIBLE STUDY AND DISCUSSION QUESTIONS

1. Did God choose those whom He would save before or after the fall? Explain your answer, providing evidence when necessary.

2. Why does God choose some for salvation but not others? Does this make Him unfair? Explain your answers.

3. Discuss the interaction of man's will and God's in John 1:12–13.

4. Explain the role of the Son as John describes it in 6:39 of his gospel.

5. How does God the Father's decision to elect some to salvation demonstrate the vastness of His love for His elect and for His Son?

6. Why does the Jesus use the metaphor of Shepherd and sheep to describe His relationship with His chosen? Use Scripture and even your knowledge of the ancient near east to answer.

7. Explain how the doctrine of sovereign election should engender humility in the heart of the elect sinner.

SUGGESTED READING FOR FURTHER STUDY

Calvin, John. *The Institutes of Christian Religion*

Horton, Michael. *Putting Amazing Back into Grace: Embracing the Heart of the Gospel*

Sproul, R.C. *Chosen by God*

Steele, David N., Thomas, Curtis C., Quinn, Lance S. *The Five Points of Calvinism: Defined, Defended, and Documented*

5

Sovereign Election (Part 2)

MESSAGE INTRODUCTION

The pain, suffering, and agony Jesus experienced during His Passion defy conceptualization. Sometimes, as Christians, we ask in our hearts, "How did He bear such a burden?" The short answer, the answer that causes tears to well up in our eyes and our hearts to swell, is love. On His way to Calgary, Jesus maintained His path and persevered on the ascent out of love for His Father and love for the ones for whom He came to die. Far from an impersonal act of selflessness, the incarnated Son of God knew each and every individual for whom He offered His body as a sacrifice, and, as Dr. Lawson demonstrates, sovereign election finds its root and meaning in this personal, amazing love.

SCRIPTURE READINGS

Jeremiah 1:5; John 1:1–18; 6:37–39; 10:1–21; 13:18; 15:16, 19; 17; Romans 9:1–27; 11:36; 1 Thessalonians 1:4; 2 Thessalonians 2:13; Titus 1:1; 1 Peter 1:1; 2 Peter 1:10

LEARNING OBJECTIVES

1. To understand God's authoritative, sovereign role in the election of sinners to salvation, a choice He made in eternity past
2. To comprehend the end of sovereign election: the glory of God and the worship of the Son, exalted on high, by His elect inheritance

QUOTATION

Do we think that we have chosen Him? If we do, we have not sufficiently recognized the depth of our own depravity or the unmerited nature of God's grace.

—James Montgomery Boice

LECTURE OUTLINE

I. God's Distinguishing Choice

    a. John 13:18: Jesus specifically singles out eleven of the apostles as chosen for salvation (with Judas excluded).

        i.   The word "chosen" refers to a choice with many possibilities

        ii. This same word for "chosen" occurs when David chooses five stones from the brook before he faces Goliath, signifying a choice among many options.

        iii. The word "chosen" occurs in a middle voice, signifying the activity on the part of the subject for the benefit of the subject.

    b. God's foreknowledge results from His foreordination.

        i.   God does not exert His will on account of his knowledge of future events.

        ii. God's eternal decree and foreordination necessitates and fosters His foreknowledge.

        iii. God does not base His choice on any future sight but out of love for Himself, His Son, and His elect (Rom. 8:29).

II. God's Purposeful Choice

    a. John 15:16: Jesus asserts straightforwardly that the choice of salvation rests in Him alone.

        i.   This election does not refer to office but every Christian's salvation.

        ii. Election, originating in God, liberates the individual and motivates him/her to serve the Lord in passionate service to His kingdom.

    b. John 15:19: Two classifications of people exist in the world.

        i.   The first classification was of the world, but Jesus plucked the individual out of the world to enter into a loving relationship with Him.

        ii. The second classification remains in the world, and for this reason lies under the tyranny of Satan and hates Christ and the truth He manifests.

        iii. This revelation should breed thankfulness and humility in the heart of the believer, for all mankind deserves death, and no one merits the free grift of grace.

III. Sovereign Election in the High Priestly Prayer

    a. John 17:2: Jesus possesses authority over *all* flesh and *all* whom the Father has given Him.

        i.   The first reference describes all of humanity.

        ii. The second reference describes the elect, further emphasizing the sovereign choice by God in salvation and eternal life.

    b. John 17:6, 9: Jesus intercedes and goes to the cross not for the sake of the world but for those who God has called out of the world.

c. John 17:24: Jesus beseeches His Father on behalf of His elect and requests that the Father might preserve them so that they might see His glory and worship Him in heaven for all eternity.

    i. The purpose of sovereign election is for the glory of God and the exaltation of the Son, who the elected saints will worship for all eternity.

    ii. This should instill joy in the heart of the believer, for nothing can compete with the privilege of worshipping our Savior in heaven for all eternity.

STUDY QUESTIONS

1. The word "chosen" that Jesus uses in John 13:18 means _____.
   a. "to choose only one possibility"
   b. "to choose out of only a few possibilities"
   c. "to choose out of many possibilities"
   d. "to choose with an intention to deceive"

2. The voice of the word "chosen" in John 13:18 demonstrates that Jesus made the choice by Himself and for Himself.
   a. True
   b. False

3. God's foreknowledge allows Him to look forward in time to evaluate if sinners will accept His call, and this affects His decision of election.
   a. True
   b. False

4. One mark of election is _____.
   a. service in God's kingdom
   b. the total eradication of sin
   c. a pompous attitude
   d. knowledge about all the mysteries of God

5. How many classifications of people exist in regards to salvation?
   a. five
   b. four
   c. three
   d. two

6. John 17 is commonly called the _____.
   a. "Intercession of Jesus"
   b. "Benedictus"
   c. "Prayer of Election"
   d. "High Priestly Prayer

7. John 17:6 demonstrates that those for whom Jesus died the Father had pre-appointed to receive the grace of the cross.
   a. True
   b. False

BIBLE STUDY AND DISCUSSION QUESTIONS

1. Why did Jesus choose Judas as a member of the twelve apostles? Explain using Scripture.

2. Does God possess foreknowledge? What pitfalls might occur when using this type of language? How does Scripture present the concept, particularly in relation to God?

3. Does the doctrine of sovereign election engender a passion within you to serve God? Should it? Explain.

4. What are some of the marks of election? Explain, and use Scripture to support your proposals.

5. What does Jesus and the Bible mean when they describe individuals as "of the world?" Refer to numerous Scripture passages for your answer.

6. How does God deal with those whom He does not elect to salvation? How do they respond to His activity?

7. Discuss the thread of God's sovereign election in John 17. Further, discuss the unbelievable love and beauty of Jesus.

SUGGESTED READING FOR FURTHER STUDY

Calvin, John. *The Institutes of Christian Religion*
Horton, Michael. *Putting Amazing Back into Grace: Embracing the Heart of the Gospel*
Sproul, R.C. *Chosen by God*
Steele, David N., Thomas, Curtis C., Quinn, Lance S. *The Five Points of Calvinism: Defined, Defended, and Documented*

6

Definite Atonement (Part 1)

MESSAGE INTRODUCTION

The Old Testament sacrificial system often causes many people a good deal of consternation. The stipulations and rituals can appear convoluted and confusing at first, second, and third glance. However, like the rest of God's revealed Word, the sacrificial system prefigured the coming of Christ and the necessity for the atonement of sin and consequent reconciliation of God. Knowing this, the sacrifices take on a whole new light and meaning, for their repetition demonstrates man's inability to meet the demands of a holy God and the inefficacy of the blood of bulls and goats. In this lesson, Dr. Lawson explains the purpose of the Levitical system, and he demonstrates from the book of John the real, effectual atonement of Christ for His elect.

SCRIPTURE READINGS

Leviticus 16; John 1:10, 29; 3:16, 17; 7:7; 12:4, 19, 31; 13:1; 17:5, 9

LEARNING OBJECTIVES

1. To understand the importance of substitutionary atonement for the doctrines of grace
2. To recognize that Jesus Christ's atonement was real and effective in paying for sins, meeting the demands of a holy God, and reconciling His people to Him.

QUOTATION

We shall not cease, dear brethren, in our ministry, most definitely and decidedly to preach the atoning sacrifice; and I will tell you why I shall be sure to do so. I have not personally a shadow of a hope of salvation from any other quarter: I am lost if Jesus be not my Substitute. I have been driven up into a corner by a pressing sense of my own personal sin, and have been made to despair of ever doing or being such that God can accept me in myself.

—Charles Spurgeon

LECTURE OUTLINE

I. Definite Atonement

    a. The doctrine of substitutionary atonement rests at the heart of the doctrines of grace.

        i. Substitutionary atonement states that Christ stepped in and bore the burden of sin for another. The question of whose sin He atoned for and what this accomplished will form the focus of the next two lessons.

        ii. The Old Testament looks forward to Christ's substitutionary atonement.

        iii. The New Testament reiterates, declares, explains, and looks forward to the benefit of Christ' substitutionary atonement.

    b. Jesus death accomplished its intent perfectly, and not one drop of His blood was shed in vain.

II. The Real Atonement of Christ

    a. The death of Christ did not potentially save, creating a contingency upon which people could decide whether or not to accept Jesus.

        i. Jesus death actually atoned for sin, reconciled the elect to God, propitiated for them, and redeemed them.

        ii. A real transaction occurred on the cross between the Father and the Son.

    b. God instituted the sacrificial system, maintained and executed by the tribe of Levi, to prefigure the coming of Christ and His atonement for sin.

        i. Our holy God must prescribe the means by which sinful man may approach Him.

        ii. The sprinkling of blood on the mercy seat on the Day of Atonement portrayed the covering of our sin and propitiation (the satisfaction of the righteous anger of God), but the scapegoat prefigured the imputation of our sins on Christ as he hung in shame upon the cross.

    c. John 1:29: John the Baptist refers to Jesus as the "Lamb of God who takes away the sins of the world." Three observations arise.

        i. Jesus definitively took sin away, unlike the scapegoat.

            1. He atoned completely for sin.

            2. He accomplished the real task of reconciliation on the cross.

        ii. The Old Testament sacrificial system applied only to the nation of Israel, whereas John the Baptist labeled Jesus as the savior of the sins of the world.

        iii. The word "world" ("cosmos") possesses different meanings depending on its context. In John, it has the following meanings.

            1. Can refer to the entire created order (1:10; 17:5)

            2. Can refer to the physical earth (13:1)

            3. Can refer to the world system governed by Satan (12:31)

4. Can refer to all unbelievers (7:7)
5. Can refer to a large group (12:19)
6. Can refer to the general public (12:4)
7. Can refer to large groups of Jews and Gentiles (1:29)
8. Can refer to the human realm (3:16)
9. Can refer to the non-elect (17:9)
10. Can refer to the elect (3:17)

d. John 1:29 refers to the elect within the groups of the Jews and Gentiles.
  i. If John the Baptist meant all of humanity, then all humanity would be saved and no one would go to hell, for God would not require an unjust second payment for sin.
  ii. Christ's atonement covers all sins of the elect, and ignoring this principle leads to an inequitable picture of God.

e. Jesus' atonement should elicit even more wonder when we recognize that He sacrificed His own divine, holy life for disreputable sinners He knows by name.

STUDY QUESTIONS

1. Jesus' death reconciled people enough to reach a state where they could decide if they would accept Him as Savior.
   a. True
   b. False

2. The one day on which the high priest entered the most holy of holies to sprinkle blood on the mercy seat was called _____.
   a. "the Day of Mercy"
   b. "the Day of Judgment"
   c. "the Day of Reverence"
   d. "the Day of Atonement"

3. The animal upon which the sins of the nation of Israel were placed, which afterwards was released into the wilderness, was called the _____.
   a. "sin bearer"
   b. "atoning animal"
   c. "goat of transgressions"
   d. "scapegoat"

4. The sacrificial system in the Old Testament applied to _____.
   a. the whole world
   b. the nation of Israel only
   c. Israel and the Canaanites
   d. the descendants of Abraham

5. The word translated "world" ("cosmos") in the book of John always has the same meaning.
   a. True
   b. False

6. If Jesus died for the sins of the whole world, referring to all humanity, then some could still go to hell.
   a. True
   b. False

7. The word "world" in John 1:29 refers to _____.
   a. The elect Jews and Gentiles
   b. all of humanity
   c. the non-elect
   d. the entire universe

BIBLE STUDY AND DISCUSSION QUESTIONS

1. What does the Old Testament say about the substitutionary death of Jesus Christ? Use specific passages of Scripture to support your answer.

2. Why does the doctrine of substitutionary atonement lie at the heart of the doctrines of grace?

3. Why can we refer to Jesus' gory death on the cross as glorious? Does this language seem offensive to you? Explain why this language and imagery is purposefully offensive.

4. Explain the purpose of the Levitical sacrificial system found in the Old Testament. Did the sacrifices actually do anything? Why or why not?

5. Why is it important that Christ truly and fully accomplished atonement on the cross?

6. What role did John the Baptist play in redemptive history? Explain.

7. If Jesus atonement paid for every sin, how would this make God inequitable? How does Scripture respond to this possibility?

SUGGESTED READING FOR FURTHER STUDY

Calvin, John. *The Institutes of Christian Religion*

Horton, Michael. *Putting Amazing Back into Grace: Embracing the Heart of the Gospel*

Sproul, R.C. *The Truth of the Cross*

Sproul, R.C. *Chosen by God*

Steele, David N., Thomas, Curtis C., Quinn, Lance S. *The Five Points of Calvinism: Defined, Defended, and Documented*

7

Definite Atonement (Part 2)

MESSAGE INTRODUCTION

The idea that God demonstrates saving grace toward a select few can rub even Christians the wrong way. Rather than responding with cries of injustice, we would do better to examine the source of these emotions. If we evaluate our hearts honestly, we will acknowledge that our feelings originate from a sense of entitlement. Simply put, as depraved human beings we believe we deserve God's mercy. Since the doctrine of definite atonement removes this notion, it receives scathing responses. Yet, as Dr. Lawson continues to show, Jesus and His Word clearly teach definite atonement, for it maintains the unity of the Godhead and demonstrates the fullness of grace absent in any other proposed system of salvation.

SCRIPTURE READINGS

Leviticus 16; Numbers 21:4–9; John 1:10, 29, 38; 3:14–17, 17; 4:42; 6:37, 39; 7:7; 10; 11:49–52; 12:4, 19, 31–33; 13:1; 17:5, 9

LEARNING OBJECTIVES

1. To understand the specific atonement Jesus Christ made for His elect
2. To recognize the unity of the Godhead in their purpose for the salvation of the elect
3. To comprehend the extent of Jesus' atonement and to whom it applies

QUOTATION

Election is ascribed to God the Father, sanctification to the Spirit and reconciliation to Jesus Christ. This is the chain of salvation and never a link of this chain must be broken. The Son cannot die for them the Father never elected, and the Spirit will never sanctify them whom the Father has not elected nor the Son redeemed.

—Thomas Manton

LECTURE OUTLINE

I. Specific Atonement in John 3:16

    a. John 3:14–15 reference the account of the bronze serpent in Numbers 21:4–9.

        i. This Old Testament pericope clearly prefigures Christ.

        ii. Salvation from death comes to the Israelites who lift their eyes to the bronze serpent raised upon a pole.

    b. John 4:42 claims Jesus as the Savior of the world.

        i. Bible unequivocally explains that not all people receive salvation and enter into His eternal rest.

        ii. Verse 42 asserts Jesus' special status as the exclusive Savior.

    c. Verse 16, then, exclaims that Jesus Christ is the only true Savior, and His love extends beyond the boundaries of national Israel to Gentiles, with no distinction.

        i. If Jesus died for the sins of all people, then God may not punish sinners for their iniquity without committing injustice.

        ii. The Bible states that God punishes the unrepentant for their sin and unbelief.

        iii. Out of an extreme depth of love, Jesus extends His atonement to all the world, not just the nation of Israel.

II. Exact Atonement

    a. John 1:38: Jesus' atonement rests in perfect alignment with the plans of the Father.

        i. The Godhead, the Trinity, works in perfect unity.

        ii. Arminianism fragments the unity of the Godhead in salvation, for it requires that each person sets out to a save a different group of people.

        iii. No division may exist in the Godhead, in nature or in person, and definite atonement maintains this harmony.

    b. John 6:39 confirms the harmony of the Godhead in their eternal purpose to secure eternal redemption for some by the cross.

    c. John 10: The Good Shepherd lays down His life for His sheep (v.11).

        i. The sheep, called by name, recognize the voice of the Shepherd (v.3).

        ii. The Father gives the sheep to the Shepherd before they recognize His voice (v.29).

        iii. Not all people belong to the Shepherd's flock (v.26).

        iv. The flock consists of both Jews and Gentiles (v.16).

        v. The Good Shepherd intentionally lays down His life for His sheep (vv.17–18).

    d. John 11:49–52: Caiaphas unknowingly confesses Jesus Christ's intercessory role as high priest and sacrificial lamb for all His elect in Israel and scattered throughout the entire world.

    e. John 12:32–33 and the surrounding context affirm Jesus' non-discriminatory atonement.

i. As already shown, the possibility of universal atonement disrupts the unity of the Godhead.

ii. The initial response of the Greeks to Jesus predicts and looks forward to their inclusion into the flock of Christ.

STUDY QUESTIONS

1. When the Lord sends fiery serpents among the Israelites as punishment for their ungratefulness and grumbling, He commands Moses to build and raise up a _____,

   a. bronze cross
   b. bronze jar of manna
   c. bronze serpent
   d. bronze dove

2. Jesus discourse recorded in John 3:16 followed from a dialogue He began with _____.

   a. Peter
   b. Zacchaeus
   c. Nicodemus
   d. Joseph of Arimathea

3. The word "world" ("cosmos") in John 3:16 refers to _____.
   a. all of humanity
   b. elect Jews and Gentiles
   c. elect Jews
   d. elect Gentiles

4. Definite atonement challenges the unity of the Godhead.
   a. True
   b. False

5. Jesus did not intend to die on the cross, but when He knew He could not overcome the external forces, He made the best of it and accepted His this course.
   a. True
   b. False

6. When Jesus says He and the Father are one, He speaks about personhood, not intention.
   a. True
   b. False

7. Caiaphas understood Jesus' role in redemptive history and voiced his support for him in John 11.
    a. True
    b. False

BIBLE STUDY AND DISCUSSION QUESTIONS

1. Describe the account of the bronze serpent recorded in Numbers 21:4–9. How does this passage prefigure and relate to Jesus Christ?

2. Explain the meaning of John 3:16. Why might some construe Christ's atonement to reach all people? How would you defend limited atonement from this passage?

3. What place does the nation of Israel have in redemptive history? Explain your answer, and use Scripture for support.

4. Why would God commit injustice if He demanded repayment for sin when Christ's atonement covered all iniquity.

5. Explain the unity of the Godhead in nature and purpose. Afterward, explain the distinction with the Godhead. Do you find this difficult to do? Should you?

6. How does Arminianism fragment the unity of Trinitarian purpose in salvation? Why does definite atonement uphold it?

7. In light of definite atonement, how must the believer respond?

SUGGESTED READING FOR FURTHER STUDY

Calvin, John. *The Institutes of Christian Religion*
Horton, Michael. *Putting Amazing Back into Grace: Embracing the Heart of the Gospel*
Owen, John. *The Death of Death in the Death of Christ*
Sproul, R.C. *The Truth of the Cross*
Steele, David N., Thomas, Curtis C., Quinn, Lance S. *The Five Points of Calvinism: Defined, Defended, and Documented*

8

Irresistible Call (Part 1)

MESSAGE INTRODUCTION

The image of conception and birth does not need much explanation. On the contrary, as human beings we understand vividly and fully the passive activity of the infant in birth. At no time does the baby possess any decision or authority in its conception or growth, but it comes into the world helpless and in total dependence on external forces. Jesus knew the power and clarity surrounding this process, and He used it metaphorically to describe the work of the Holy Spirit in regeneration. As Dr. Lawson demonstrates in this lesson, Jesus, and John through Him, leaves no ambiguity process of salvation: God carries out His sovereign will in salvation, and spiritually dead hearts, like a baby, cannot contribute or refuse.

SCRIPTURE READINGS

John 1:12–13; 3:3–8; 17:2, 9, 19, 24; 19:30

LEARNING OBJECTIVES

1. To recognize the full affirmation of definite atonement in the gospel of John
2. To receive an introduction to the fourth doctrine of grace, the irresistible call, and to understand the early references to it in John's gospel

QUOTATION

Restore us to yourself, O Lord, that we may be restored!

—Lamentations 5:21a

LECTURE OUTLINE

I. Final Thoughts on Definite Atonement
    a. John 17
        i. Verse 2: the usage of "all"
            1. The first usage of "all" refers to humankind in general.
            2. The second usage of "all" refers to the elect.
            3. Christ came into the world to give life to the elect, not all flesh.
        ii. Verse 9: Jesus' specific intercession
            1. As a priest entering the Holy of Holies, so Jesus prays before His Father.
            2. He clearly demarcates His salvific work for the elect, not for the world.
        iii. Verse 19: Jesus sets Himself apart as the sacrificial lamb for the elect, the same group for which He has interceded throughout this prayer.
        iv. Verse 24: Christ's death on the cross and the Father's love for His Son from eternity past results in the incorporation of the elect in the worship of God forever.
    b. John 19:30
        i. Jesus' last words on the cross ("It is finished.") refer to the completion of His mission to ransom the elect.
        ii. Having paid the price for sin in full, Jesus merits His full inheritance: the elect.
        iii. Christ triumphs in death, and not one of His sheep will escape His grasp.

II. Irresistible Call
    a. John 1:12–13
        i. Regeneration of the heart enables an individual to receive the free offer of the gospel (2 Corinthians 5:17).
            1. Regeneration does not occur through lineage.
            2. Regeneration does not occur through human effort.
            3. Regeneration does not occur through man's will.
            4. Regeneration occurs by the sovereign choice of God.
        ii. John clearly affirms a monergistic regeneration, in which God alone quickens the dead spirit unto life.
    b. John 3:3–8
        i. The metaphors of water and wind refer to the Holy Spirit.
        ii. While the water washes and cleanses, the uncontrollable wind blows wherever and whenever it will.
        iii. Similar to the untamable nature of the wind, Jesus uses the metaphor of birth to demonstrate that human beings play no part in their

regeneration. Just as a child cannot resist being conceived and brought into the world, so too a dead heart cannot ignore or reject the work of the Holy Spirit.

STUDY QUESTIONS

1. The two usages of the word "all" in John 17 refer to the same group of people.
   a. True
   b. False

2. Jesus' sacrifice on the cross results in the ability for individuals to accept or deny His call to repent and believe.
   a. True
   b. False

3. The Greek word *tetelestai* is a financial term meaning _____.
   a. "paid in part"
   b. "debt removed"
   c. "paid in full"
   d. "account liquidated"

4. Regeneration occurs through _____.
   a. genetic lineage
   b. human effort
   c. the will of man
   d. the sovereign work of God

5. The Arminian position on regeneration concludes that God and man work _____ in regeneration.
   a. monergistically
   b. synergistically
   c. antagonistically
   d. telepathically

6. The metaphors of water and wind refer to the work of the Father.
   a. True
   b. False

7. The metaphor of birth in regards to regeneration emphasizes the role of parents in the conversion of their children.
   a. True
   b. False.

BIBLE STUDY AND DISCUSSION QUESTIONS

1. What three offices does Jesus Christ hold? How does He function in each one?

2. Explain the purpose of the High Priestly Prayer. Explain how its time of deliverance affects its impact.

3. How might someone defend universal atonement in the face of John 17? How would you respond?

4. Why is Jesus called the Lamb of God?

5. What does it mean to be "born again"? How does this occur? Cite and explain various Scripture passages in your answer.

6. Explain the difference between monergistic and synergistic regeneration. Which does the Bible espouse? Why?

7. Explain why John uses the metaphors of water and wind in reference to the Holy Spirit.

SUGGESTED READING FOR FURTHER STUDY

Calvin, John. *The Institutes of Christian Religion*
Hodge, A.A. *The Atonement*
Horton, Michael. *Putting Amazing Back into Grace: Embracing the Heart of the Gospel*
Owen, John. *The Death of Death in the Death of Christ*
Sproul, R.C. *The Truth of the Cross*
Steele, David N., Thomas, Curtis C., Quinn, Lance S. *The Five Points of Calvinism: Defined, Defended, and Documented*

9

Irresistible Call (Part 2)

MESSAGE INTRODUCTION

Popular culture generally depicts sheep as cuddly, peaceful animals. Yet, those who have spent even a small amount of time around sheep know that they are stubborn, wayward, smelly, and sometimes even vicious. This truth makes Jesus' comparison to His followers as sheep all the more poignant. We, as sinners, possess all of these qualities, some in more abundance than others. Yet, the analogy finds its most power in our Good Shepherd's willingness to know us personally, to ensure our safety, and to bring us to His Father's house. As Dr. Lawson explains in this lesson, the call of Christ to follow Him, applied by the Holy Spirit, exhibits such amazing grace and kindness that it should pull our heartstrings perpetually.

SCRIPTURE READINGS

Psalm 23; John 1:12–13; 3:3–8; 5:25; 10:1–5; 11; 17:2, 9, 19, 24; 19:30; Acts 11; Romans 8:29–30; Ephesians 2:1, 8–9; Philippians 1:29; Hebrew 12:2

LEARNING OBJECTIVES

1. To understand the power and irresistible nature of the call of the Holy Spirit to believe in Jesus Christ.
2. To recognize the deeply personal aspect of Jesus call to His sheep.

QUOTATION

Irresistible grace is not irresistible in the sense that sinners are incapable of resisting it. Though the sinner is spiritually dead, he remains biologically alive and kicking. As Scripture suggests, the sinner always resists the Holy Spirit. We are so opposed to the grace of God that we do everything in our power to resist it. Irresistible grace means that the sinner's resistance to the grace of regeneration cannot thwart the Spirit's purpose. The grace of regeneration is irresistible in the sense that it is invincible.

—R.C. Sproul

LECTURE OUTLINE

I. Irresistible Call

    a. John 5:25: Spiritual resurrection

        i. Coming to faith in Christ involves the resurrection unto life and belief of a spirit dead in its trespasses.

        ii. Like the resurrection of Lazarus, man cannot breathe life into his dead spirit, but only divine power can bring regeneration (John 11).

        iii. Repentance and faith follow the Holy Spirit's work of regeneration.

    b. John 6:37–44: Spiritual drawing

        i. The Holy Spirit must draw individuals that the Father has chosen to Christ.

            1. The Greek word for "draw" in this passage means "to drag by force."

            2. The draw of the Holy Spirit occurs in conjunction with the new heart He places in the individual.

        ii. This activity on the part of the Holy Spirit is sovereign, supernatural, and irresistible, bringing depraved men into the fold of Christ.

    c. John 10: Sovereign calling

        i. Verse 1: Jesus refers to the religious leaders of Israel in His days as "robbers" and "thieves" because they did not own the "sheep" of Israel.

        ii. Verses 2–4: Jesus, the Good Shepherd, receives free passage into the sheep pen from the gatekeeper, wherein He calls to His sheep (believers), and they respond to His voice.

        iii. Jesus' flock never dwindles or lessens, but all His sheep (Christians) will arrive home at the throne of God.

STUDY QUESTIONS

1. The resurrection of Lazarus represents man's cooperation with God in exercising faith in Jesus.

    a. True

    b. False

2. Regeneration of the spirit pales in comparison to God's creation of the physical universe.

    a. True

    b. False

3. The Greek word used in John 6:44 for "draw" means _____.
   a. "to make a mark"
   b. "to attract"
   c. "to drag by force"
   d. "to enliven"

4. Jesus referred to the religious leaders of Israel in His day as _____.
   a. "pirates"
   b. "robbers" and "thieves"
   c. "hustlers" and "gamblers"
   d. "gladiators" and "mercenaries"

5. John 10 identifies who as the gatekeeper to the sheep pen?
   a. Peter
   b. John the Beloved
   c. Moses
   d. John the Baptist

6. Christians, also referred to as "sheep," may leave the flock and forget the voice of their master, Jesus.
   a. True
   b. False

BIBLE STUDY AND DISCUSSION QUESTIONS

1. How does the resurrection of Lazarus in John 11 resemble the work of God in salvation?

2. Can the free call of the gospel be rejected? Is this call equivalent to the call of the Holy Spirit? Explain.

3. Why did Jesus refer to the religious leaders of Israel in His day as "robbers" and thieves"? Should the people of Israel have recognized this? Explain.

4. Describe, if you can, the moment you received the irresistible call of the Holy Spirit to believe in Jesus Christ?

5. Can children receive the call of the Holy Spirit and not have any memory of it? Must your recollection of this call be "clear as day"? Explain.

6. Does this image of Christ calling out to you by name seem personal? What does this demonstrate about the nature of salvation?

SUGGESTED READING FOR FURTHER STUDY

Calvin, John. *The Institutes of Christian Religion*

Horton, Michael. *Putting Amazing Back into Grace: Embracing the Heart of the Gospel*

Steele, David N., Thomas, Curtis C., Quinn, Lance S. *The Five Points of Calvinism: Defined, Defended, and Documented*

10

Preserving Grace (Part 1)

MESSAGE INTRODUCTION

The idea of eternal security acts as a huge stumbling block for many people. When human beings honestly assess their own desires and motives, the wickedness witnessed clearly paints a bleak picture. Yet, this reality makes God's grace all the more amazing. That He loves and walks alongside His elect despite their shortcomings and rebellions demonstrates His deep love and kindness. Rather than befuddle us, as Dr. Lawson argues in this lesson, this grace should drive us to praise our glorious God for His sovereignty and mercy in salvation. Nothing can snatch us from His hand, no matter how hard we, or others, might struggle subvert His plan and providence.

SCRIPTURE READINGS

John 3:15–18, 36; 4:13–14; 5:24; Romans 1:18; 8:1, 23; 1 Peter 3

LEARNING OBJECTIVES

1. To understand the blessed eternal ramifications delivered through true belief in Jesus as Savior.

QUOTATION

"When I heard it said that the Lord would keep His people right to the end, I must confess that the doctrine of the final preservation of the saints was a bait that my soul could not resist. I thought it was a sort of life insurance, an insurance of my character, an insurance of my soul, an insurance of my eternal destiny. I knew that I could not keep myself, but if Christ promised to keep me, then I should be safe forever."

—Charles Spurgeon

LECTURE OUTLINE

I.   Persevering Grace and Eternal Life
    a.   John 3:15: Whoever believes in Christ will have eternal life.
        i.   The verb "have" in this verse refers to a present reality and condition, not to the future.
        ii.   Eternity reaches into this life.
            1.   The reference to eternal life in this verse pertains to the quality of life, for communion with God begins with regeneration, repentance, and faith.
            2.   The reference to eternal life in this verse also pertains to duration of life, a life never-ending.
    b.   John 3:36: Belief in Christ
        i.   Belief in Christ involves the mind, heart, and will.
            1.   An individual must consciously know and recognize their lost condition before they believe in Jesus.
            2.   The heart must be persuaded by the truth of the gospel.
            3.   The will must make the decisive choice to repent of sins and to surrender to Jesus.
        ii.   Belief in Jesus brings eternal life.
    c.   John 3:16: Whoever believes in Christ will not perish.
        i.   By perish, Jesus assures the Christian that he will never experience the wrath of God, but he will receive His love for all eternity.
        ii.   Although blunders and slip-ups may occur, nothing can rip a Christian from the love and security of God.
    d.   John 4:13–14: The life-giving water Jesus offers (Himself) quenches the spirit eternally, meeting a spiritual need that physical water can never supply.
    e.   John 5:24: Never condemned
        i.   Jesus promises that believers will not experience judgment by God.
        ii.   The righteousness of Christ is imputed to believers, and for this reason they may stand justified before the Father for all eternity.

STUDY QUESTIONS

1.   The truth of persevering grace has no bearing on the previous four doctrines of grace.
    a.   True
    b.   False

2.   Eternal life begins when an individual dies and goes to heaven.
    a.   True
    b.   False

3. The reference in John 3:15 to "eternal life" pertains to duration only.
   a. True
   b. False

4. Before an individual can possess saving faith in Jesus, he must consciously know that he is lost.
   a. True
   b. False

5. John 3:16 promises that a Christian will _____.
   a. never experience suffering
   b. not taste physical death
   c. never receive the wrath of God
   d. fade into oblivion eventually

6. The act whereby God declares sinner righteous on account of Christ's righteousness is called _____.
   a. justification
   b. sanctification
   c. atonement
   d. glorification

BIBLE STUDY AND DISCUSSION QUESTIONS

1. When does a Christian receive eternal life? Explain.

2. How does the answer to the previous question affect the Christian mindset and daily living?

3. Explain the roles of the mind, heart, and will in belief in Jesus Christ. What other aspects of the individual must be involved in belief? Defend your answer with Scripture.

4. Do Christians have multiple conversion experiences? Explain. How would you counsel a Christian who believes he or she must constantly dedicate himself or herself to the Lord?

5. Does John 3:16's encouragement that believers will not perish include earthly suffering? Explain. If suffering remains a part of the Christian life, why do Christians experience pain and sorrow?

6. How can believers stand in the presence of God, especially since we continue to sin even after our regeneration?

SUGGESTED READING FOR FURTHER STUDY

Calvin, John. *The Institutes of Christian Religion*

Horton, Michael. *Putting Amazing Back into Grace: Embracing the Heart of the Gospel*

Parsons, Burk, ed. *Assured by God*

Steele, David N., Thomas, Curtis C., Quinn, Lance S. *The Five Points of Calvinism: Defined, Defended, and Documented*

11

Preserving Grace (Part 2)

MESSAGE INTRODUCTION

The example of Judas Iscariot sometimes causes us to scratch our head. How could someone so close to Jesus possibly betray Him and receive the label "son of perdition." Wouldn't the acts, words, and nature of Jesus instill in Him a true sense of worship, awe, and adoration? Simply put, the answer is "no." As the rich man discovered in the parable of Lazarus, even the miraculous nature and works of Jesus cannot convince a sinner dead in his transgressions about His Messianic role without divine intervention in the heart. As Dr. Lawson shows in this lesson, this decision rests in the sovereign will of God alone. Yet, when God determines to pluck someone from his depraved state, He will not be thwarted and His work will never be undone. On the contrary, the recipients of God's mercy will persevere in grace throughout eternity, eventually arrayed around the throne of their magnificent, glorified Savior, Jesus.

SCRIPTURE READINGS

John 3:15–18, 36; 4:13–14; 5:24; 6:39, 44, 54; 10:27–29; 11:25–26; 14; 16–17; 17:12, 24; Romans 1:18; 8:1, 23; 1 Corinthians 6:19; 1 Peter 3

LEARNING OBJECTIVES

1. To understand the eternal security promised and enacted by Jesus and described in the book of John.
2. To appreciate the careful concern and guard Jesus gives to His flock as the Good Shepherd, the result of which will be their worship of Him enthroned on high.

QUOTATION

"Christ is not the guardian of our salvation for just one day or even for a few days, but He will care for our salvation to the end."

—John Calvin

LECTURE OUTLINE

I. Persevering Grace
    a. Never lost
        i. John 6:39: Jesus will lose none of those given to Him by the Father.
            1. This promise issues from before the foundation of the world.
            2. It aims at resurrecting the dead on the last day, and Christians will worship Him in glory for eternity.
        ii. John 6:44, 54: These verses reaffirm the eternal security granted by the sovereignty election of God.
    b. Forever secure
        i. John 10:27–29: No one will snatch the sheep from the hand of Jesus.
            1. Jesus may have had in mind both the religious leaders of Israel as well as demonic powers, particularly Satan.
            2. Their attempts are futile.
        ii. John 10:28–29: The power of the divine Lord of creation assures the veracity of this promise.
    c. Never die
        i. John 11:25–26: No believer will suffer eternal death.
            1. Jesus uses definite articles to demonstrate that belief in Him alone offers eternal life.
            2. Even if physical death occurs, a believer can be confident he will never suffer eternal death, physical or spiritual.
        ii. Unbelievers will experience the "second death": the eternal condemnation and banishment to hell.
    d. Never abandoned
        i. John 14:16–17: Jesus provides the Holy Spirit to dwell within Christians forever.
            1. This act ensures the eternal perseverance of believers.
            2. In conjunction with this, the Holy Spirit continues to clean and sanctify believers more and more in the image of Christ.
    e. Never unguarded
        i. John 17:12 Jesus explains that He has been guarding the disciples, by which they have persisted in Him.
            1. Jesus kept them from apostatizing and falling away.
            2. Judas, despite His proximity to Jesus and His teaching, was never saved. On the contrary, as the son of perdition, God ordained Judas to betray Jesus and receive condemnation.
        ii. John 17:24: Jesus intercedes for His flock that they might witness His in His full glory forever. His prayers do not go unanswered.

STUDY QUESTIONS

1. Persevering grace is known also as _____.
   a. persevering mercy
   b. grace unfettered
   c. perseverance of the saints
   d. stumbling at the finish line

2. Satan has a real chance to snatch the children of God out of the hands of Christ.
   a. True
   b. False

3. The work of persevering grace in salvation involves the _____.
   a. Father only
   b. Son only
   c. Holy Spirit only
   d. three persons of the Trinity

4. When Jesus offers eternal life, He means that believers will never suffer
   _____.
   a. physical death
   b. physical and spiritual death
   c. any pain whatsoever
   d. permanent physical death and spiritual death

5. All people will suffer a second death.
   a. True
   b. False

6. "Ichabod" means "the glory has departed."
   a. True
   b. False

7. The "Helper" referred to by Jesus in John 14:16 is _____.
   a. Himself
   b. the Father
   c. the Holy Spirit
   d. the Word of God

8. Judas exemplifies the principle that an individual can lose his salvation.
   a. True
   b. False.

BIBLE STUDY AND DISCUSSION QUESTIONS

1. Does persevering grace seem unfair to you? Unfair for whom? Explain.

2. Can an individual not believe in persevering grace/eternal security and still be a Christian? Explain.

3. Why might a professing Christian deny the doctrine of persevering grace?

4. How might Satan attempt to snatch Christians away from the hand of Jesus? If Satan knows the promise and power of God, why does he still try?

5. Explain the different roles the three persons on of the Trinity in salvation. How do they work in conjunction with each other?

6. What does Dr. Lawson mean by "second death"? Who experiences this?

7. Explain the guarantees achieved by the indwelling of the Holy Spirit. How does the Holy Spirit dwell in a Christian.

8. Why did Judas betray Jesus? Explain your answer in light of Jesus' words in John 17.

SUGGESTED READING FOR FURTHER STUDY

Calvin, John. *The Institutes of Christian Religion*

Horton, Michael. *Putting Amazing Back into Grace: Embracing the Heart of the Gospel*

Steele, David N., Thomas, Curtis C., Quinn, Lance S. *The Five Points of Calvinism: Defined, Defended, and Documented*

12

This Changes Everything!

MESSAGE INTRODUCTION

Not all Christians accept the doctrines of grace. They believe the Bible presents a different picture of salvation, one in which the will of man exercises itself to the exclusion of God's sovereignty. Sadly, the picture more often than not encourages a lower view of God and a heightened view of man, which never leads to any positive outcome. As Dr. Lawson explains in this final lesson of the series, the doctrines of grace should lead Christians into a greater understanding and appreciation of their great, gracious God and His creation. Any other response would contradict the doctrines of grace themselves.

SCRIPTURE READINGS

Read the gospel of John in light of the lessons learned in this study.

LEARNING OBJECTIVES

1. To understand and appreciate the transforming power and acceptance of the doctrines of grace brings in the life of a believer

QUOTATION

A truly humble man is sensible of his natural distance from God; of his dependence on Him; of the insufficiency of his own power and wisdom; and that it is by God's power that he is upheld and provided for, and that he needs God's wisdom to lead and guide him, and His might to enable him to do what he ought to do for Him.

—Jonathan Edwards

LECTURE OUTLINE

I.   Dr. Lawson's Background

    a.   Dr. Lawson did not grow up in a church that taught the doctrines of grace, but he was raised in a Wesleyan Church that adhered to the Arminian doctrine in regards to salvation.

    b.   He resisted them and argued against their veracity, even after beginning his studies in seminary.

    c.   This lesson explores his transformation of understanding and his acceptance of the doctrines of grace.

II. Dr. Lawson's Journey of Affirmation of the Doctrines of Grace

    a.   Overwhelmed

        i.   When Dr. Lawson finally recognized the role of God's mercy and grace in his salvation, he experienced an overwhelming feeling at God's immense grace.

        ii.   Whereas before he felt as if he was doing God a favor in his decision to attend seminary and enter ministry, he now experienced an extreme humility.

        iii. The doctrines of grace, when viewed properly, should engender a deep meekness in the hearts of believers, for they demonstrate the sovereign grace of God in the unmerited and depraved life of a sinner.

    b.   Explosion of love

        i.   When Dr. Lawson finally accepted the doctrines of grace, his love for God burgeoned immensely.

        ii.   While saved before accepting the doctrines, when the Holy Spirit moved within him to affirm these truths, a passion ignited within him like never before.

        iii. When a believer recognizes the immense mercy and grace involved in these doctrines, he cannot help but feel a deep, powerful love for His caring, good God.

    c.   Illumination of Scripture

        i.   When Dr. Lawson grasped the veracity of the doctrines of grace, the Bible became alive to him.

        ii.   No longer did he need to "re-explain" passages like Romans 9 and Ephesians 1, but God's sovereignty leapt out at every page to him. He witnessed this gladly.

        iii. When a believer accepts the doctrines of grace, he cannot help but witness their presence and power throughout the entire Word of God.

    d.   New confidence in ministry

        i.   These doctrines infused Dr. Lawson with new confidence in his ministry.

      ii. He finally understood God's activity around him, preparing hearts to receive the gospel.

      iii. The doctrines of grace supply confidence for all involved in ministry and in God's kingdom. They remove the unbearable burden of saving sinners from spiritual death and recognize God's complete sovereignty.

  e. Greater compassion for the lost

      i. Dr. Lawson finally experienced a true compassion for unbelievers trapped in their sinful nature.

      ii. Unbelievers are totally helpless, and this should heighten the desire of a Christian to minister to them.

  f. A new depth of fellowship with other Christians

      i. Dr. Lawson experienced a new sense of camaraderie both with extant believers who shared his conviction, but also with believers who had gone before him.

      ii. All Christians should experience a fellowship with and love for one another, but accepting the doctrine of grace increases the believer's understanding of God's sovereignty throughout creation and time, which in turn provides a level of connection among God's people less available in other doctrinal positions.

  g. A heightened sense of missions

      i. Like George Whitefield, Dr. Lawson felt the call and ability to go into the entire world and deliver the gospel to God's elect.

      ii. The doctrines of grace demonstrate the importance of the gospel reaching all the ends of the earth, for His elect remain spread throughout creation and no place is too dark to be pierced by the light of His truth.

  h. Increased sanctification

      i. Dr. Lawson began to be more earnest about his walk with the Lord. He realized God has called him to a great purpose, and he could not give into the snares and traps of this world.

      ii. Recognizing the sovereignty of God in salvation should heighten our appreciation for our Lord and increase our desire to imitate Jesus as we serve Him in His kingdom.

  i. Higher view of worship

      i. A higher view of God and His sovereignty created a higher view of worship for Dr. Lawson.

      ii. When recognition of God's transcendence and majesty blossoms in the heart of the believer, increased adoration cannot help but follow.

STUDY QUESTIONS

1. Accepting the doctrines of grace as biblically sound and derivative should engender a cool, unemotional, academic faith.

     a. True

     b. False

2. Only a few parts of Scripture deal with the doctrines of grace.
    a. True
    b. False

3. The doctrines of grace free us from the burden of evangelizing to others.
    a. True
    b. False

4. Understanding the doctrines of grace should ignite greater compassion in our hearts for the lost.
    a. True
    b. False

5. William Carey engaged in missions because he believed men and women around the world needed the opportunity to reject the irresistible call of the Holy Spirit when they heard the Word of God preached.
    a. True
    b. False

BIBLE STUDY AND DISCUSSION QUESTIONS

1. Why do people respond polemically to the doctrines of grace? Can an antagonistic response be reduced to one simple cause?

2. Why should the doctrines of grace create humility on the heart of a Christian? Do we sometimes war against this, even after regeneration? What can we do to prevent this?

3. Do the doctrines of grace engender a deeper love in your heart for God? Why?

4. Does the entire Bible proclaim the doctrines of grace? Attempt to find their place in each book of the Bible.

5. How might the doctrines of grace instill confidence in believers when they work for the kingdom? How do they affect your confidence?

6. How do the doctrines of grace supply greater compassion in the hearts of believers for the lost?

7. Do the doctrines of grace offer greater Christian fellowship for you with those around you and those who have come before you? Why or why not?

8. How do the doctrines of grace affect your view of missionary work? For the better of for the worse? Why?

9. How has an understanding of the doctrines of grace caused you to imitate Christ more closely?

10. Does a proper appreciation of God's sovereignty and transcendence affect your worship? Why or why not?

SUGGESTED READING FOR FURTHER STUDY

Calvin, John. *The Institutes of Christian Religion*

Horton, Michael. *Putting Amazing Back into Grace: Embracing the Heart of the Gospel*

Sproul, R.C. *What Is Reformed Theology?*

Steele, David N., Thomas, Curtis C., Quinn, Lance S. *The Five Points of Calvinism: Defined, Defended, and Documented*